S. S. BAZINET

VAMPIRES SUCK BUT YOU DON'T HAVE TO

Renata Press
Albuquerque, New Mexico

Published by Renata Press
Website: RenataPress.com
Author website: SSBazinet.com

ISBN 978-1-937279-00-4

Acknowledgments

My deepest appreciation goes to Laura Christine, my beloved, genius editor. She's always a guiding light. I am so grateful for Anna Marie, and for her input, wisdom, and continued support. A big "thank you" goes to Julia Ann. Her thoughtful guidance, counsel, editing and recommendations are the best. I am so grateful Gabriel. Whenever I stray, he insists on gently turning me back in a positive direction. Many thanks to Gene for his editing skills. I truly value his loving dedication to detail. I am so very blessed to have all my family and extended family! They are always there for me, no matter what the circumstance.

Contents

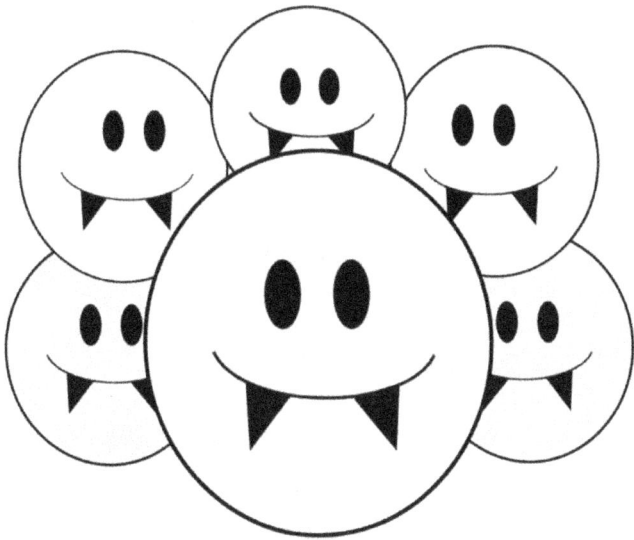

The needy-feedy world!

We were happy as kids. What happened?

When many of us think about being a child, we think about having fun and being happy. When we think about being an adult, we think about taking care of our needs. We have exchanged our happiness for *neediness*.

We live in a needy world.

We live in a world of neediness. We live with vampires who feed off of each other's life force and energy. The funny or not-so-funny thing is that we don't recognize the vampires around us. In fact, when we look in the mirror, there might be a vampire staring back at us. We're so conditioned to accept the neediness in ourselves and others, we don't notice it. But it's there. It's always there. So are the vampires. So is our craving.

Is being a vampire a permanent condition?

No. Once we understand how we became vampires, we can reverse the process. The vampires walking this earth are not dead. Their heart may be in a prison of sorts, but it's alive and waiting to be set free. That's what this little book is all about. *It's time to reclaim ourselves.*

How do we leave our vampire ways behind?

There are two rules for those who choose to leave their neediness behind.

1. You shall not suck on others.

2. You shall not let others suck on you.

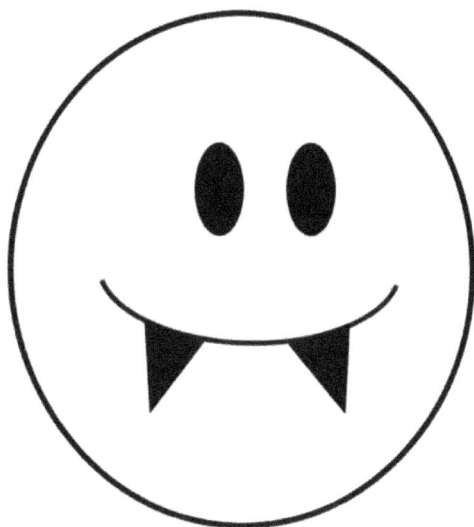

"Sorry, are my fangs showing?"

What is a vampire?

A *vampire* is a person who feeds off of, or consumes from an external source. In our discussion, we are defining a vampire as someone who feeds off of the *life force* or *energy* of others. Vampires are sometimes referred to as *suckers*.

Who are the vampires in this world?

They might be you and me. Being a vampire is a normal, daily *condition* for most humans.

Why are we vampires?

We *believe* that we need to feed off the energy of others in order *to survive.*

Are we vampires at heart?

No.

Is this an artificial condition?

Yes, we learn to be this way. We're taught that feeding off of others is a necessary part of life.

Why don't we think of ourselves as vampires?

Very few of us contemplate who we truly are. We accept the definitions we're given as children. If we do what we're taught, we think of ourselves as basically 'good' people. We're satisfied with that label.

What are the signs that we live in a vampire world?

When we observe the people around us, we notice that they are constantly stressed and exhausted. Many come home at night with just enough energy to eat and then drop down in front of the television. They're "drained."

How can I tell if I'm a vampire?

Any of us could be a king size vampire and not know it. There is a way to tell. We begin to notice our interactions with others. Are people genuinely happy to see us coming? Do they look forward to taking our calls? After we've been around friends, family, and coworkers, do they still look happy? Are they smiling or do they stare back with blank faces?

We have to be objective when we ask ourselves these kinds of questions. We might be so used to people fading away before our eyes that we're oblivious!

What if it's not obvious, could I still be a vampire?

Yes. Many vampires fly under the radar. They're subtle about how they feed and how much life force they extract from others. We call them 'sippers.' They take a little sip of energy here or there. For example, they might smile and ask us about something as innocent as the clothes we're wearing. "You look great, but is that the right color for you?" That simple question places a doubt in our psyche. We frown and agree that we might not look our best. What's actually happening is that we're focusing on the other person, thinking that we need their validation. In exchange, we give them a bit of our energy. *Any time there is an exchange and someone feels bad after the exchange, that sucks!*

But if we are the vampires, why do we feel drained?

Unless one is at the top of the food chain, we are expected to donate a good portion of our life force to others without a lot of fuss. It's part of our training.

What if I don't want to be a sucker?

We'll be discussing the answer to that question and others in the following chapters.

We apologize if this information makes you feel bad.

We aren't here to make you feel guilty. If you realize that you're a sucker and wish that you weren't, try to comfort yourself with the fact that *you and many like you don't want to suck!*

VAMPIRES SUCK BUT YOU DON'T HAVE TO

That's what this little book is all about – *we can get our fix without sucking*!

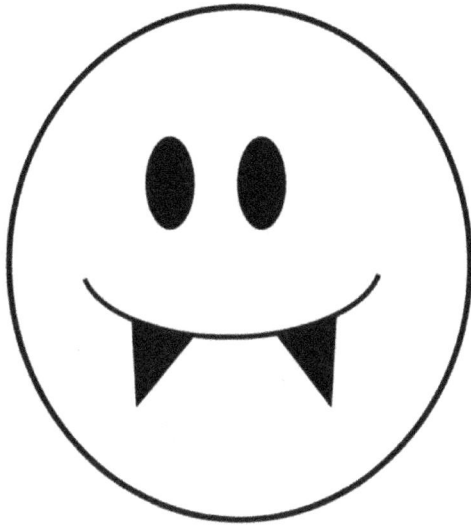

"I'm nice, really I am!"

How did it all start?

As soon as children are old enough to give someone their attention, they have already learned the basics. They have learned to focus outside of themselves.

What happens next?

As we learn to focus outside of ourselves, we begin to forget about who we really are on the inside. The more we forget about who we are, the more important the external becomes. We begin to manipulate the external aspects of life to get what we want. A baby learns that if he screams loud enough, someone will bring him a bottle or change his diaper or entertain him.

So where does the problem come in?

Babies are helpless. They have to have external assistance. The problem is that many times we grow up still *feeling* like a powerless child. We maintain the rules and regulations we've been taught. Now, they keep us stuck in a way of life that is *needy*. We continue to depend on the external for our needs and for validation. This conditioning sets up mental and emotional constructs that define who we think we are. For example, we think and feel like we need someone to love us. We have forgotten that we can be fulfilled by loving ourselves. We forgot how to *self-sooth* and *self-nourish*.

Why didn't somebody help me to feel capable and self-soothing?

First of all, our parents, teachers and the people who influenced us were usually good-intentioned. However, most of them felt needy themselves. *They couldn't teach what they didn't know.* Instead, they taught us how to satisfy our needs externally. They taught us how to succeed by being a consumer. In many cases the word, consumer, is a nice word for vampire.

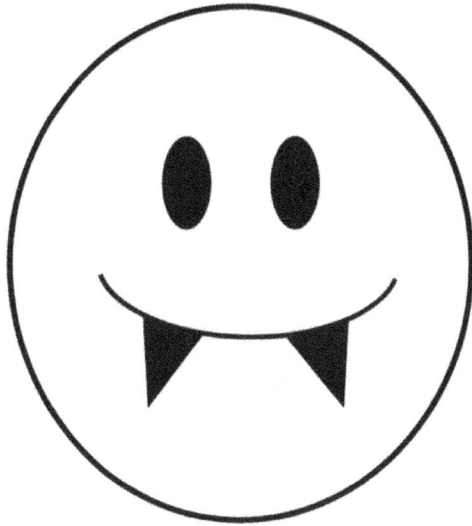

"What's on the menu?"

What is meant by the phrase "getting your fix?"

"Getting your fix" refers to the act of feeding on the energy or life force of someone outside of ourselves. It means that we're getting energy from an external source.

What does it feel like to have someone feed off of us?

After someone feeds off of us, we feel "less than" before. Our emotions take a dip. Our smile disappears. Many times we look for an opportunity to "feed" on another person so that we can feel better. If nobody is around, we often consume food as a substitute for our emotional, energy needs.

What does it feel like to feed off of someone?

After we extract energy from someone, we feel more empowered for the moment. But it's like a physical meal, we soon get hungry again. The good feeling is temporary.

How many ways are there to feed off of another?

There are *countless* ways to extract energy from others. We are all experts in the art of sucking. Listed below are a few of the most common examples of how people extract energy:

> **Playing the victim**
> **Bullying**
> **Preaching**
> **Being judgmental**
> **Talking incessantly**
> **Acting superior**
> **Teasing**

We'll examine a few of these common, "sucky" methods and see how they work. Remember, when people use these methods to extract energy from others, many times, the other person turns around and finds a way to return the favor. The *sucker* becomes the *suckee*! When that happens, life can then be summed up with this simple statement. "I feed, you feed, we all feed on each other."

"Hurting me is going
to cost you!"

The victim type of vampire – are you their next meal?

Vampires often use guilt to try to make others give them what they want. They're the ones who are easily hurt and make sure that we know about it. Even unintentional slights are made to seem serious. Sometimes, it feels like they're saying, "You drove a stake through my heart, you cruel beast! Now you have to pay for your actions. Feed me!"

But that's not really going to work. When we exchange our energy with someone, it's like giving them a blood transfusion with the wrong type of blood. A victim type might think we can help to satisfy their needs, but we can't. *We can not fix another person.*

Besides, we are not here to use our energy to feed each other. When we encounter a victim, we have to remember the second rule. *You shall not let others suck on you.*

What can we do to help others who play the victim role?

We can believe in them. We can see them in a brighter light that says, "I see you as okay, therefore, I also believe you aren't really a victim. You've just forgotten who you are, a capable person, who *thinks* they need the energy of others. In truth, you need to believe in yourself."

"Everyone wants
a piece of me."

Are you playing the victim?

Sometimes we feel like victims. We come away from an encounter with someone, and we feel like we've been sucked dry. When this happens, it's very important not to try to make the "sucker" pay for their crime. That reaction keeps us in the vampire cycle. Instead, *we have to learn to stop giving others power over us* in the first place. That's what we mean when we say, "You shall not let others suck on you."

But how?

When we learn how to give our *attention* to our own powerful self, it helps to break the victim cycle. We'll be discussing the process in the later chapters of the book. So please hang in there. We can truly reverse the process of giving away our energy.

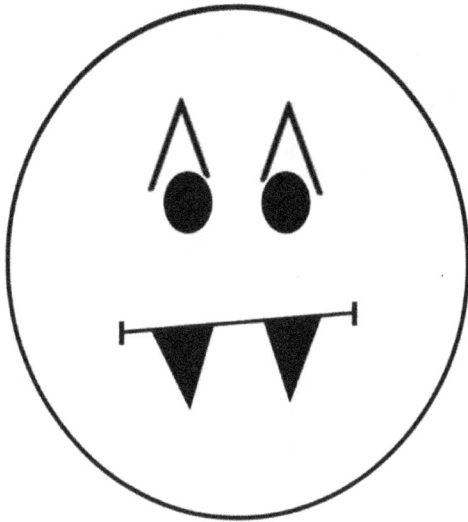

"Hand over some
energy or else!"

Why is the bully vampire so scary?

Just hearing the word *bully* usually gets a
reaction. We know what's coming. A bully gets
his fix by intimidation or show of strength. As
children, we learn that a bully can take many
roles. The bully could be a parent, a teacher, or a
classmate. In the adult world, the bully could be
a spouse, a boss, a friend, or an acquaintance. If
allowed, a bully can "suck you dry."

How do people become bullies?

Let's look at the bully from a *needy* point of view. As a child, the more we look to the external for our survival, the more we forget about the real us, the *heart* of who we are. The *bully* scares us because we sense her/his *great need* for an external fix. Where is the real person under that bully exterior?

When we view a *bully* as a *needy person*, it gives us a different perspective. Hopefully, that perspective will help us to stand our ground and believe in ourselves enough to refuse the bully.

"I know what's best,
and I best snack!"

Preacher in the house! Please, not another sermon!

We all know what a preacher is. They are people who are bent on telling us something, whether we like what they're saying or not. Preachers come in a variety of models. There are the red faced, fist pounders. There are the frowning, "You better do this or else" types.

When preachers speak, *their tone and bearing are meant to get our full attention.* When they convey *their truths*, our eyes go wide because we have that feeling that *an authority has spoken*. Do we dare refuse them our focus or our energy?

Supposedly, preachers are looking out for us, trying in some way to *save* us from a bad relationship, or too much drink, or a variety of other *sins* that they see when they look at us. But if they are on our side, why do we go away feeling sapped by their message?

A preacher type of person can actually be a *needy* individual.

The easiest way to see preachers as energy vampires is to compare them to a person who isn't a vampire. Think of someone you like to be around, a person who encourages you, a person who points out your good qualities. They help you to trust yourself and to make better decisions for yourself. In other words, *they are helping you to refocus your attention inward*. They are helping to reverse the process that made you a vampire in the first place.

Preachers often suck up energy by scaring us. Many times, they can be bullies who use words and advice to get our energy.

Note: A *helpful* person encourages us to look *inside* ourselves for security and a sense of well being.

An *energy vampire* encourages us to look *outside* ourselves for security and a sense of well being.

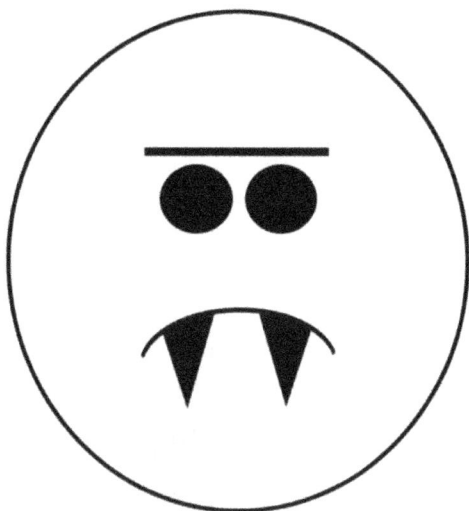

"The bad shall be
snacked on!"

Here comes the judge!

We all make judgments. We decide what tastes good and what tastes bad. Judgment is a part of our lives. But what happens when another person *judges us*? What happens when they decide that our lives are a part of their courtroom?

"Don't eat that. It's not good for you."

"You need to exercise more!"

"You're being ridiculous!"

A judgmental type of vampire makes statements that let us know what's right and what's wrong for us and for our life.

How does a judgmental vampire get another person's energy?

The first thing they do is pull us *outside* of ourselves. They encourage us to rely on the *external* for validation. When we *need* external validation, *we* are willing to *pay* for it. We lose or forget more of who we are. Our connection to the real us, the person inside, is weakened. We become someone else's puppet.

Many times, if we become *the puppet, we also start to play the victim*. We extract energy in many covert ways, maybe not with the judge, but with others we come in contact with.

When it comes to making a judgment about the "art of judging others" or "having others judge us," judgment sucks!

"Look at my amazing
photos of my grass!"

Cover your ears, it's the yapper!

The incessant talker, or yapper, gets energy by
babbling on and on. Sometimes, they butt into
conversations, demanding a bit of the good
stuff, our energy. Others are extremely docile in
appearance and technique. They wait for their
moment to corner us at the office or at a party.
They are the *quiet yappers*. Some quiet yappers
use their monotonous drone to glue us to the
spot as they tell us about their grass. Other
yappers are always excited. They grab our

attention with their frequent, enthusiastic outbursts.

Whatever their method, yappers are good at what they do. The person being *yapped at* sometimes experiences a feeling of paralysis. It's often accompanied by desperation as they realize how quickly their life force is being consumed.

Note: Some yappers avoid eye contact. They wouldn't want to have to disconnect their direct feed into a vein.

So how do I get away from a yapper?

Use the second rule. "You shall not let others suck on you."

In truth, we are not helping the person by being their victim. With that in mind, realize that the yapper is in her/his own spell. They are often totally externalized. Secondly, realize that all of us are probably yappers now and then. Have compassion for this boring, but very effective feeder.

What if I'm a yapper who is going on and on, and I don't know how to stop?

When we find ourselves *yapping*, there's a simple solution. We need to close our mouth and put on a little "Mona Lisa" smile. It will let people know we've come to our senses. Next, it's a good time to congratulate ourselves for stopping our own "suck" party.

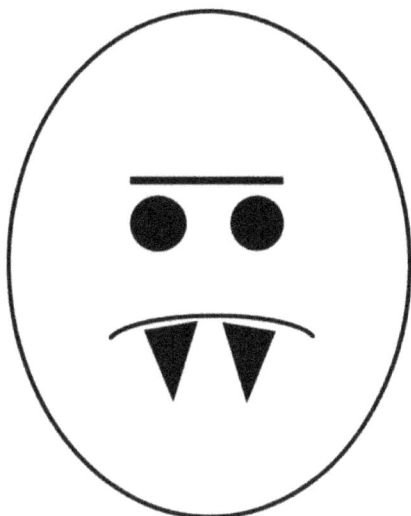

"It's simple. I'm better than you!"

What about the superior vampire?

Many times we willingly give away our energy by putting people on a pedestal. They are usually people who are rich, famous and/or powerful. When we're around them, we sometimes try to "suck up" to them. But we know that we are not in charge. If they turn around and want a "piece" of us, we usually give it to them.

Why do we look up to them?

Many times we've learned to feel this way. We overhear our parents and others discussing the "important" people. We're presented with ads, news clips, and movies depicting their importance. We think they are superior in some way that deserves our "attention." But when we give others our energy, we're robbing ourselves of our life force.

What's the solution?

Bring your attention back to yourself. Give yourself a chance to "star" in your own life!

"Please stop laughing at me!"

What's the problem with teasing?

Teasing often starts in childhood. We are teased by our siblings and/or supposed friends. Sometimes we are teased by parents, relatives or teachers. Their wily remarks may seem innocent, but are we uplifted by the sport? No. Teasing is a form of shaming. That's why our face turns red.

Yet, the message is clear. We are supposed to be good sports. We are told not to act like a baby.

"Just give up a little energy, please, and don't make it a big deal."

The problem is that sometimes there is so much teasing, we feel so diminished, so drained, that we can lose all sense of self confidence.

When it comes to teasing, there's a very simple bottom line. *Teasing sucks.* Period.

"Are you as hungry as I am?"
"Yep, it's time for a snack."

What about friendly snacks?

Sometimes, when we are "in need," we approach friends for a little "pick me up." We might meet for coffee or a drink. We might call someone for a chat. Once we settle into a conversation, we engage in a recital of our woes.

What we're actually doing is fishing for that supportive energy that we feel we need. It's not that we're trying to be a sucker, we just want to stop feeling bad.

Many times our friend then proceeds to expound on all the things that are wrong in their life. Their need is similar to ours. We end up "supporting" or "feeding" each other.

In this situation, both parties know the routine. We each play our needy roles in a friendly sort of "my turn, your turn" exchange of energy.

These friendly meet-ups become feeding sessions for both parties. But here's the question, does either party come away feeling better? Perhaps, especially if we feel we're not alone, that we're not the only sucker around.

The encouraging thing to remember is that there's a better way to feel fulfilled and satisfied with ourselves and our lives.

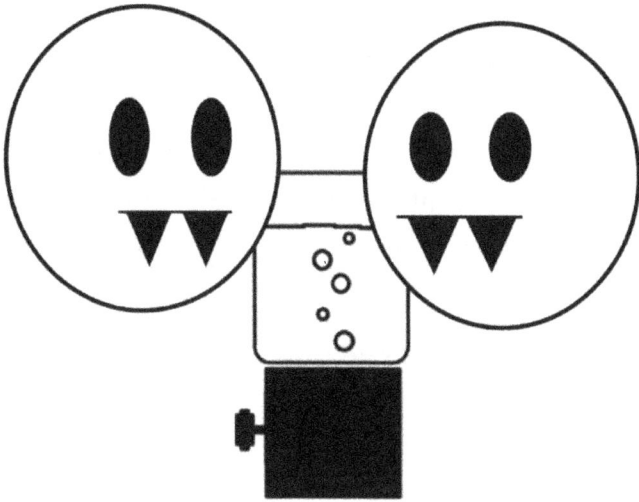

"Does work suck, or is it just me!"

Work can be a vampire hangout.

We often label our place of employment as *work*. We dread Mondays! But why are we so anxious for five o'clock to come each weekday? There are lots of reasons.

Co-workers can be sucky in a variety of ways that we've already talked about. Some can be victims who always have something to complain about. Others can be so tedious that we literally want to fall over after a conversation.

Bosses can make demands for a small amount *or* a great deal of our life force depending on just how hungry they are. On the other hand, if we become a feeding-frenzied employee, we can prove so obstinate and difficult that our boss ends up a husk trying to get us to do something. It "works" both ways.

Organizations can suck too!

If we belong to an organization, the test is always the same. Does our organization leave us feeling better or worse?

"We found each other!"
"Yes, let the feasting begin!"

Why are relationships such a big deal?

We need outside relationships because we never learned how to care about and love the person inside. We look to the outside and other people for our sustenance.

What happens when two people, who are really vampires, form a relationship?

In the first phase of a vampire relationship, most of us keep our fangs to ourselves. We put our best *foot* forward when we're getting acquainted with someone. (A foot isn't nearly as scary as a fang.) Unfortunately, the honeymoon usually ends as soon as we feel the other party is okay with our foot. It's now time to expose a little more of ourselves. The word, *need*, creeps into our relationship. We begin to express what we *need* from our partner. They do the same with us. That's when the arguments start.

Arguments can become great feeding fests. Maybe that's why there are so many of them. When we are low on energy, we often look to our partner to provide an energy snack. Almost any topic can be used to get things going. "You forgot to put the top on the toothpaste!"

The problem with snack time is we are not the only one who's hungry. Our needy partner knows how to extract energy too. As we argue with each other, the words and fangs are fast and furious. Many times, both parties come away drained. Most vampire relationships end in misery because we think the other person will make up for the deadness that we feel inside. When our partner fails to "live up to" our expectations, the relationship "goes down the tubes."

Truly glorious relationships exist between people who know how to satisfy themselves.

They are connected to their own vitality and thriving life force. They come together to share experiences, not to feed off of one another. We all have a chance for that kind of glorious relationship, but first, we have to stop being suckers.

"Tell me the truth, Doc,
am I dead?"

Vampires sometimes feel dead inside!

As vampires, we often feel lifeless and drained of joy. Our childhood days of living with enthusiasm and excitement are long gone.

Why is a vampire's life so tiresome, so devoid of true joy?

Our *heart* isn't in anything we do. Instead, our externally focused mind is in charge. Its chatter is directive and all consuming. It uses its data bank of facts and experiences to keep us focused on survival, on getting that "fix."

What about the vampire's heart?

When living in this externally focused condition, we don't connect with our heart very often, not in a sustained and lasting way. We don't feel any personal, empowering life force surging inside of us. But no matter how "dead inside" we might *feel*, the truth lives on. The heart is always behind the scenes! On a physical level, nature is set up to provide for our needs, to give us the energy that we require. Our heart is alive and working constantly, whether we know it or not. Here are a few facts about our physical heart.

Average heartbeats per day: about 100,000 or about 35,000,000 per year. Average miles that our blood travels per day: about 12,000 miles. In an average lifetime, our heart pumps about 1 million barrels of blood.

Our joyful, good-feeling, *emotional* heart is there too. It fueled the laughter of our childhood, and it continues to fuel every genuine smile. Every moment of our lives, it pumps us full of energy. Others can see that vital energy in us! It's the fix that the vampires around us want. *Now we have to want ourselves.*

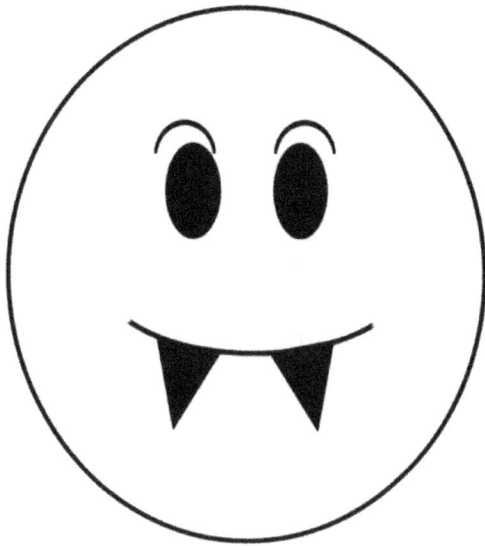

"You have my attention."

What if I give up my vampire ways?

Vampires suck, but we don't have to! We have what we need inside of us.

Other vampires recognize our inherent energy and life force. How would they feed on us if we didn't have those things? Now it's time for us to understand something very important. We can *be* someone's meal ticket. We can make someone *our* meal ticket. But there's a third choice. We can forget the whole vampire scene and nourish ourselves.

We *lost touch with ourselves* as we attached ourselves to the outside world. But the bottom line is that *we never lost the real us.* That person is just hidden from view, waiting to be rediscovered.

But how do we rediscover ourselves?

The way back to ourselves is contained in one word, attention.

A definition of *attention*: to focus the mind on something or someone.

We start our wonderful journey back to ourselves by turning our attention inward. We *learned* how to give our attention to what was outside ourselves. We *learned* how to be and act like other people, but the cost for that learned behavior was huge. *We forgot who we are.* We *learned to give away bits of our identity* because we were taught that it was the price of survival. But we are not helpless children anymore. As adults, we can make a decision to reclaim who we are.

"I'm all about being me!"

When we refocus our attention, who or what will we find?

At first, it might be a little difficult to know *who we really are*. Our mind keeps us busy with facts and strategies for surviving. However, remember that we *did know* ourselves a long time ago. *Our baby self was very focused within.* Once its basic needs were met, its world was self-contained. It laughed when it wanted to laugh, and it cried when it wanted to cry. Our baby self crawled over to a stack of blocks or other toys and played by itself. Our baby self didn't worry about any obligations to the outside world. It was already interacting with things, but in a happy, self-centered way.

Mom, Dad, grandparents, and many others had to teach us to maintain a constant focus on the world of *others*. It was a big job! In the beginning, they used rattles and cooing sounds to get us to look at them. They clapped their hands. They clapped *our* hands. They played peek-a-boo with us. As we got older, they encouraged us to play with other kids in the sandbox or the playground. They did their best to socialize us.

Dictionary.com's definition of the word, socialize: make fit for life in companionship with others.

Our parents and teachers went to all that trouble because they wanted us to *"fit in."* They didn't want us to end up a *misfit* or loner.

All the people who instructed us about the world were part of the process. They gave us *their* best ideas about what the world is all about. As we grew up, these *facts* filled our *minds* and structured our view of life. In the end, it all worked! As adults, our *minds give us constant feedback* that is based on our *external focus and conditioning.*

But there is another aspect of *who we really are* that doesn't get nearly as much attention. That part is expressed by our *heart* or our *feeling nature.* When we were born, it's the *unique us* that we brought into the world.

"I don't have to wait to feel good!"

What's so great about a person's "feeling nature?"

If we didn't have a feeling nature, we couldn't *feel good*. And let's face it, almost everything we want, whether it's a relationship or a new car, we want because we *think* it will make us feel good.

When the mind is in charge, we associate feeling good with something we left behind, "the good old days," or something we can achieve in the future. We ping-pong back and forth between those two illusory worlds.

The real you and me can feel good here and now just as we did as a baby or a child.

A baby is a feeling being. Babies know when they feel good and when they don't. When they're happy, they enjoy that *feeling state* immediately. They don't wait for the future.

Our feeling nature, our heart, is our connection to the present moment.

When we bring our attention and our focus back to our feeling self, we don't have to wait for something in the future in order to feel good now.

"Is this supposed to be a nose?"

Why is there a picture of a nose on this page?

We are attempting to illustrate one of the most important tools that we can use to reconnect to ourselves. It's called breathing.

When we *focus* on taking a deep breath, we *deliberately* bring more life force into our body. But that deliberate act does more for us. In that brief moment, we shut out any *externally* focused thoughts! How? Our mind can only process one thought at a time. If we take several *intentional*, deep breaths, we buy some time. In those few moments, we have the opportunity to begin our journey back to ourselves. As we focus and breathe, we can begin to establish a new pattern of thought. For example, "I intend to experience being the real me right now!"

We can also concentrate on happiness itself. Happiness and our hearts naturally go together when we let go of our external thoughts. External thoughts are structured and restrictive. Heartfelt happiness flows!

Why is happiness so elusive?

Many people *think* and *plan* and *work* very hard to *have* material success and power, yet they don't *feel* happy when they succeed. One reason is that happiness is *not* a thought or an objective. Happiness is a *feeling*. It's a *state of being* that's always available. We don't have to wait for it. Happiness is accessed within. *Our hearts generate all feelings of happiness.*

How can we bring our attention back to the state of being happy?

Here's an exercise that might help. As we breathe and relax, let's focus on something that makes us smile. It could be the most beautiful rose we've ever seen. Or we might focus on a pet and how cute and adorable it is. We could entertain visions of waterfalls and woodland scenes.

If our mind wanders during the exercise, we can pause and think about our nose again. We can bring ourselves back to the moment with another conscious breath.

Once we're able to shift to a happy feeling state, let's enjoy the gift that we've given ourselves. Let's bask in our contented feeling for as long as we can.

What if we can't find that moment of happiness?

Sometimes, when happiness eludes us, we need to sooth ourselves. We need to remind ourselves that it takes practice to let our hearts flow. Many of us have associated the heart with feelings of hurt. Reversing that process takes patience. We have to remind ourselves that we are sometimes taking baby steps back to who we really are.

"I love my bag of tricks!"

What else can we do to refocus on ourselves and connect to the feeling of happiness?

We were all born with our bag of tricks, the things that make our hearts sing! That's why as children, we know how to play without anyone teaching us what to do. We know how to run and laugh for the pure joy of it. That bag of tricks is still inside of us. We just have to go on a treasure hunt to find it. Once we find it, we can look inside and examine the contents.

We each have a unique way of being who we are. What makes one person laugh isn't funny to another. For some, dance music is great. For others, a quiet walk in the woods does the trick. So it's up to each of us to find what pleases us, to find that playful, simple joy that we knew as children.

And because our joy is contained in our hearts, each night we can pause and have a wonderful thought. Whether or not we used our bag of tricks that day, it's okay. We can remind ourselves that beyond our treasure hunt for ways to enjoy ourselves, our true bliss is always there inside of us, waiting for us to dip into its warmth.

"Wow! I forgot how great a body can be!"

Can our body help us bring our attention back to us?

Sometimes we forget the wonders of having a body. We're so busy seeing its faults that we forget how great it is. Without a body, how could we smell a rose or feel our soft, warm blanket? How could we hear our favorite music or watch the sun rise? So, let's remember that if we want to bring our attention back to us, we have to include our body in the mix. Conscious breaths can help us connect to our physical *being* and remember how amazing it is.

What about exercise and eating?

Exercise often becomes that laborious job that sucks. We sometimes only exercise out of duty. But exercise can be fun and a great way to connect with ourselves. Walking in the park is exercise. Gardening is too. Dance is a fun exercise that can be squeezed into tiny spaces of time. Five minutes away from the desk is long enough to listen to a great rock song that gets us moving. The important thing is to find a few minutes to *refocus on us*. Exercising our body, doing something we like, can be a great way to do just that.

When it comes to food, we can make a date *with our body* for lunch or dinner. Even if it's just once a week, we can sit down and nurture our body with our attention. Like a date with a friend, we can talk over anything that's not working. We can come up with new ideas about how to make life with our body more fun.

The biggest gift we can give our body is to stop our mind from entertaining critical thoughts. Instead, we can learn to give our body the gift of attentive nurturing.

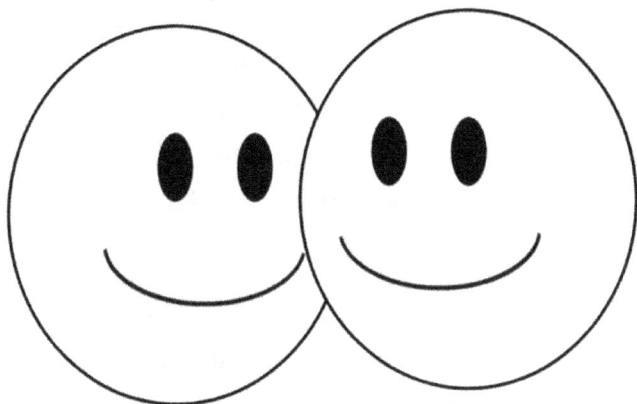

"I like the word 'fun'!"
"Me too! Let's have fun together!"

How can a word like "fun" help me?

When someone says, "Let's have fun," we instantly perk up, even if it's just for a moment. Good feelings and words often go together. They're a perfect way to bring our attention back to us. So let's find a favorite word, one that makes us smile inside. When we take a moment to breathe, we can think about 'our' word and let a good feeling bring us back to ourselves.

What about the words that suck?

Certain words are draining. For example, words like ugly, bully, and bad, bring up feelings that we don't enjoy. Some words can be very powerful if we let them pull our attention away from who we are, from that heartfelt place inside of us. So we must learn to be careful about the words we use and the words that dominate our thoughts.

One more last question! What about interacting with people in our lives who are still caught up in an external focus? What about the people who suck?

When we interact with others who are *still sucky*, we have to come from a place of self-nurtured security. If we do that, at least *we* won't suck! And that's the point, isn't it? Vampires suck, but we don't have to!

* * *

Thank you for reading this little book. If you enjoyed it, please tell your friends. Word of mouth is an author's best friend. ~ S. S. Bazinet

www.ingramcontent.com/pod-product-compliance
Lightning Source LLC
Chambersburg PA
CBHW020518030426
42337CB00011B/451